Look Out!

A Story About Safety on Bicycles

Written by
Cindy Leaney

Illustrated by
Peter Wilks

Rourke

Publishing LLC
Vero Beach, Florida 32964

Before you read this story, take a look at the front cover of the book. Matt and Emily are on their bicycles.

1. How are they practicing bicycle safety?

2. What is different about the boy riding behind them?

Produced by SGA Illustration and Design
Designed by Phil Kay
Series Editor: Frank Sloan

www.rourkepublishing.com

Library of Congress Cataloging-in-Publication Data

Leaney, Cindy.
   Look out! : safety on bicycles / by Cindy Leaney ; illustrated by Peter Wilks.
      p. cm.-- (Hero club safety)
   Summary: When Emily, Makayla, Jose, and Matt go bicycling, they witness what can happen if you do not wear a helmet.
   ISBN 1-58952-744-5
   [1. Bicycles and bicycling--Safety measures--Fiction. 2. Safety--Fiction.] I. Wilks, Peter, ill. II. Title.

   PZ7.L46335Lo2003
   [E]--dc21

2003043237

Printed in the USA
MP/W

Welcome to The Hero Club!
Read about all the things that happen to them.
Try and guess what they'll do next.

www.theheroclub.com

"Mom, I'm leaving for the park now."

"Have you got everything?"

"Yes, lunch, water bottle, mitt, and helmet."

"Okay. Have fun."

4

"Hi, Mrs. Johnson. Is Makayla ready yet?"

"Hi, Emily. Yes, she'll be right down. Are you going the usual way?"

"Yes."

"Okay. See you later."

"Are you guys ready?"

"Yeah. José is just saying good-bye
to his mom. Here he comes."

"Right. All set?"

"Yep. Let's get going."

9

"Oooh. I wish I had a dorky helmet."

"Me, too."

"Watch it!"

"Are you okay?"

"I think so."

"Is he okay?"

"He's knocked out. He's unconscious."

"We need an ambulance. I'll call 911."

"He didn't see that wood sticking out. He rode straight into it."

"He's unconscious. We better call 911."

"We already did."

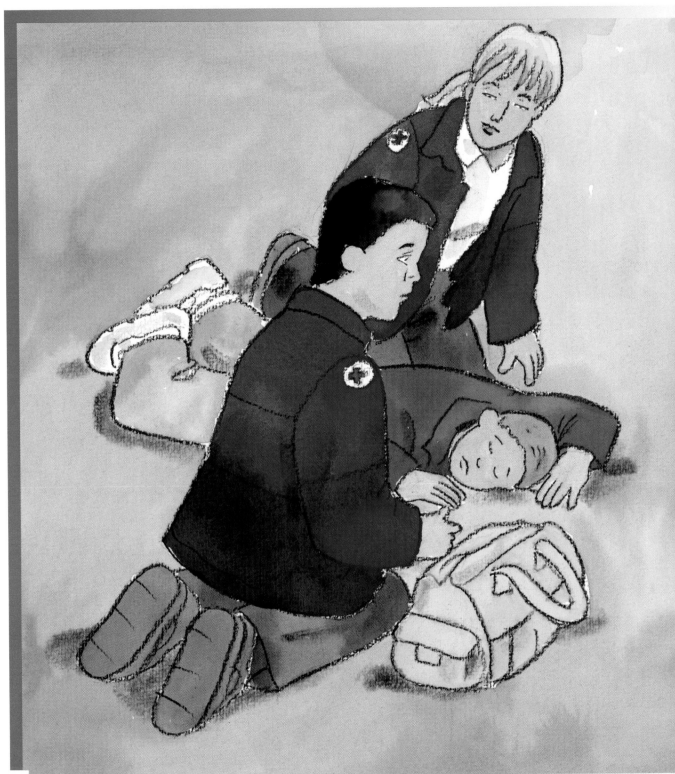

"You didn't move him. That's good."

"Okay, we'll take it from here.
We're going to need a board for
his back."

"Is he going to be all right?"

"It's hard to say. It could be serious.
He wasn't wearing a helmet."

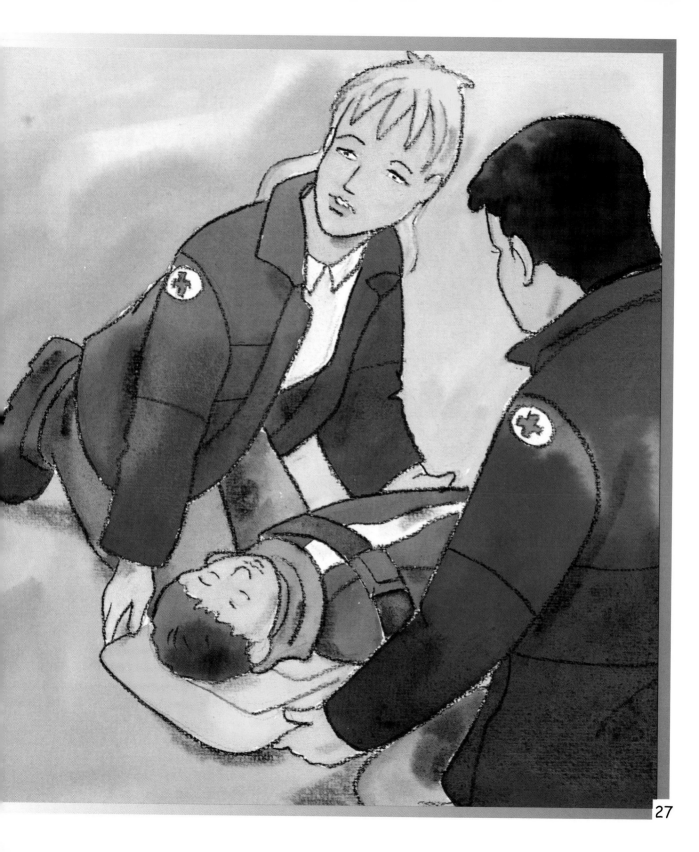

"Thanks for coming. Tom has something he wants to say to you kids."

"I'm sorry we made fun of your helmets. It was stupid of us. And thanks for calling 911."

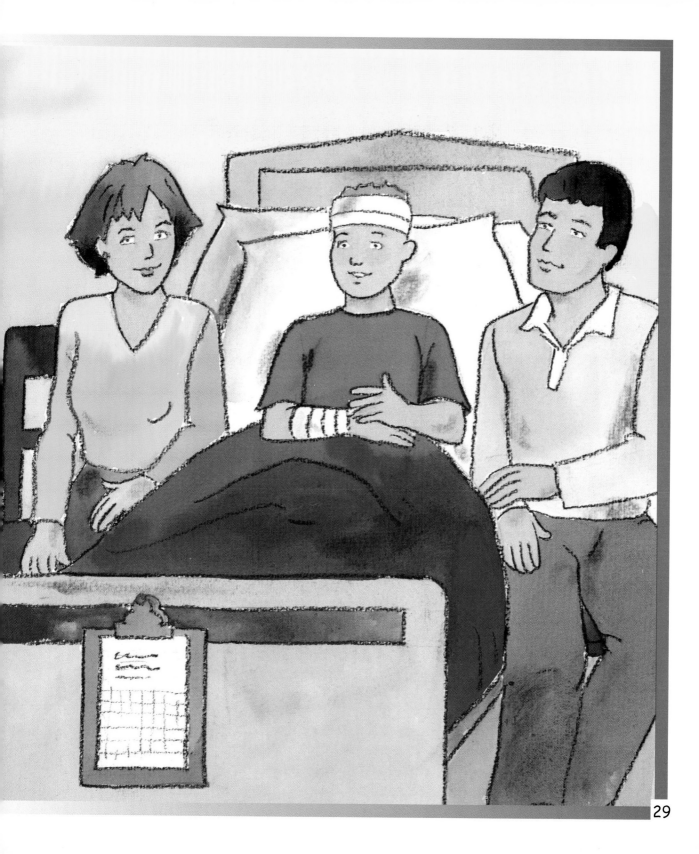

WHAT DO YOU THINK?

Was it a good idea for Emily, José, Makayla, and Matt to just keep riding, even when the other kids made fun of their helmets?

Why or why not?

IMPORTANT IDEAS

What did the Hero Club Kids do to stay safe on their bikes?

What do you do to stay safe on your bike?

Now that you have read this book, see if you can answer these questions:

1. What does Emily have with her when she sets off for the park?

2. How do the Hero Club kids call an ambulance?

3. The Hero Club kids didn't move the injured rider. Was this a good thing?
    Why or why not?

4. How does the injured rider thank the Hero Club kids?

About the author

Cindy Leaney teaches English and writes books for both young readers and adults. She has lived and worked in England, Kenya, Mexico, Saudi Arabia, and the United States.

About the illustrator

Peter Wilks began work in advertising, where he developed a love for illustration. He has drawn pictures for many children's books in Great Britain and in the United States.

HERO CLUB SAFETY SERIES

Do You Smell Smoke? (A Book About Safety with Fire)

Help! I Can't Swim! (A Book About Safety in Water)

Home Sweet Home (A Book About Safety at Home)

Long Walk to School (A Book About Bullying)

Look Out! (A Book About Safety on Bicycles)

Wrong Stop (A Book About Safety from Crime)